MY BIG BOOK OF BABY animals

FOG CITY PRESS

Table of Contents

Amazing Baby Animals

With their cute faces, big eyes, and playful antics, baby animals are just so adorable! We choose animals such as puppies and kittens as pets and enjoy looking after them and watching them grow.

Farms are a good place to see all kinds of baby animals, including fluffy chicks and ducklings and cuddly lambs and baby goats. Sometimes you will see newborn foals and calves taking their first steps on legs that look too big for their bodies.

Baby animals born in the wild are cute critters, too. Luckily, most of them are well cared for by their parents until it is time for them to look after themselves. Read on to find out all about their fascinating stories.

Pets & Farm Animals

Baby animals are everywhere. Cats, dogs, and other pets share our homes, and farm animals live all around us.

Cats

Baby cats are tiny when they are born, but they grow fast. Fluffy, cute, and cuddly, kittens are full of energy. They love to play with one another. Sometimes they play at fighting. Chasing things is fun, too. Kittens even chase their own tails!

Kittens are usually born together with brothers and sisters.

Even when they are small, kittens play at hunting. This little guy is watching and ready to pounce.

Like grown-up cats, kittens have long whiskers. These help them feel their way around in the dark.

ALL ABOUT

Kittens

Time mother pregnant: 60–67 days

Number born at a time: 1–12

First food: Milk

Dogs

Puppies are cute! Several brothers and sisters are born at the same time, one after another. This is called a litter. Some dogs are smaller than others. The smallest puppies could fit in your hand. Puppies grow up to be loving and faithful pets.

This puppy has long ears and big brown eyes. Would you like to pet him?

Puppies stay near their mother. When they get older, they will
12 stay close to their owners.

Puppies love to play, run, and jump. This little fellow is raring to go. See him run!

ALL ABOUT

Puppies

Time mother pregnant: 61–65 days

Number born at a time: 2–17

First food: Milk

Rabbits

Rabbits are soft and cuddly. Most live in the wild, but they also make great pets. Tame rabbits love being stroked. An outdoor house for tame rabbits is called a hutch. Wild rabbits live in groups underground in large burrow systems called warrens.

These baby bunnies have tall ears, but some rabbits have soft, floppy ears.

Like puppies and kittens, baby rabbits are born in litters, with brothers and sisters.

Baby rabbits are called kits. Once kits stop drinking milk, they eat grass and other plants.

ALL ABOUT

Rabbit Kits

Time mother pregnant: 29–35 days

Number born at a time: 2–12

First food: Milk

Geese

Geese live on land, but they spend a lot of time in the water. They are large birds with long necks. When they hatch, they are covered in fluffy down. Before they can fly, they need to grow adult feathers. They don't need adult feathers to swim, though.

This gosling is stretching his wings. It will be weeks before he can fly.

Goslings love to swim. They paddle with their webbed feet.
They can swim quickly.

ALL ABOUT

Goslings

Number
of eggs:
2–12

Time to hatch:
21–30 days

First food: Grass

These goslings
are staying close
to their mother.
She will show them
where to get food
in the pond.

These little birds get going quickly. Baby chicks are able to walk, see, eat, and drink!

Just Hatched!

Baby chickens are called chicks. They hatch from eggs after developing for about three weeks. Once their feathers dry, chicks follow their mother around, pecking at anything that looks tasty. Like their mother, chicks feed on young grass, insects, and other tasty morsels.

Chicks are covered in fluffy, soft feathers called down.

1 I am inside my egg growing bigger every day. I need to be kept warm and cozy.

2 It's time to break out. I am using a special egg tooth on my beak to crack the shell.

3 I'm free! My egg tooth has dropped off my beak. My feathers are dry and fluffy.

Some chicks are white. Others are yellow. When they grow up, they will look like their parents.

ALL ABOUT

Chicks

Number of eggs:
4–19

Time to hatch:
20–22 days

First food:
Plants and insects

Chickens

Chickens are farm animals, but some people keep them as pets. Chickens hatch from eggs one at a time. As soon as the chicks hatch, they make cheeping noises. They are covered in soft, fluffy feathers and can find their own food straight away.

Baby chickens have sharp beaks they use to pick up seeds and bugs.

Young chicks huddle together under their mother's wings for warmth and protection.

Ducks

Baby ducks are usually yellow at first, but they can be white, brown, or black. Ducklings can walk and swim within hours of hatching. Like most baby animals, they follow their mother wherever she goes. This is the best way to stay safe.

This mother duck is taking her ducklings down to the water.

Ducklings are good swimmers because they have webbed feet. They easily keep up with mom!

Ducklings cheep before they can quack. Female ducklings learn to quack before their brothers.

ALL ABOUT

Ducklings

Number of eggs:
8–13

Time to hatch:
27–28 days

First food:
Plants and insects

Goats

Baby goats are adventurous animals, like their parents. They love climbing and jumping around. Kids are usually born in the spring when there is plenty of grass to eat. Most goats have hairy coats, but some breeds of goats have woolly coats.

Even little goats have long ears. They can wiggle them around.

Male goats fight by head-butting. These kids are practicing for when they're older!

Nanny goats produce milk for their kids to drink. Male goats are called billy goats.

ALL ABOUT

Kids

Time mother pregnant: 145–155 days

Number born at a time: 1 or 2

First food: Milk

Llamas

Llamas are farm animals that come from the mountains of South America. They are related to camels, but they have no humps. People use them to carry things and spin their wool to make yarn. You might see one at a petting zoo.

Baby llamas, or crias, have thick, fluffy fur to keep them warm.

A baby llama stays close to his mother. She makes a humming sound to keep her baby calm.

Once baby llamas have stopped drinking their mother's milk, they eat grass and other plants.

ALL ABOUT

Crias

Time mother pregnant: 340–350 days

Number born at a time: 1 or 2

First food: Milk

This foal is just a few days old. She is staying close to mom, so she can drink milk when she wants to.

ALL ABOUT

Foals

Time mother pregnant: 340–350 days

Number born at a time: 1 or 2

First food: Milk

Horses

Baby horses are called foals. They have very long legs and learn to walk within hours of being born. Soon they are running fast, which helps them get strong. Ponies are small horses. Sometimes people see adult ponies and think they are foals.

This foal is taking a rest. Sometimes horses sleep standing up.

Young foals have shorter tails than adult horses. This foal's tail will grow longer soon.

This little guy has already got his first bridle. Bridles are straps used to attach reins for riding.

First Steps!

Foals are quick to get up on their feet. Like many hoofed animals, they can run within a day of being born. In the wild, they need to be able to keep up with their mothers and run away from dangerous animals such as wolves or mountain lions. Wild or tame, all foals are fast runners.

A foal's legs are nearly as long as they will be when they are grown.

1 I have just been born in a stable, and I am taking my first breaths.

2 Although I am less than an hour old, I can already stand. I am a bit wobbly!

3 Only a few hours old and I am standing tall. Soon I will be running outside with mom!

Pigs

Adult pigs may not look cuddly, but baby pigs are cute little critters. Baby pigs grow up with a litter of brothers and sisters. Piglets play together and like to run around in their pen. The last baby pig to be born is usually the smallest and is known as the runt.

Piglets often snuggle up or jostle with their brothers and sisters.

Like many baby animals, piglets sleep a lot. All that play makes them feel very tired!

ALL ABOUT

Piglets

Time mother pregnant: 112–115 days

Number born at a time: 6–14

First food: Milk

Piglets have big ears that they can move and round noses called snouts.

Sheep

Lambs are usually born in spring, just as the weather starts getting warmer. Lambs are full of energy. They love to run and jump in fields of fresh, green grass. They live in flocks with their mothers and with other mother sheep and lambs.

Sheep usually give birth to just one lamb, but sometimes they have twins.

Lambs stay close to their mothers, especially when they are very young.

This little lamb is growing his first coat of wool. Wool is used by people for making clothes.

ALL ABOUT

Lambs

Time mother pregnant: 144–151 days

Number born at a time: 1 or 2

First food: Milk

Highland cows come from the hills of Scotland. Even the calves have long fur to protect them from the cold.

ALL ABOUT

Calves

Time mother pregnant: 278–289 days

Number born at a time: 1 or 2

First food: Milk

Cows

Calves are strong babies. They can stand up within hours of birth and run when they are only two days old. Just like you, they drink milk. It makes them grow. Most of the milk we buy in stores is cows' milk that has been put into cartons or bottles.

This calf is curled up for a rest. He is lying on a soft pile of straw.

These two calves are white and brown. They will stay the same color all their lives.

Born to Run

Some babies get up on their feet quickly. They can walk within hours of being born and are soon able to run alongside their moms. This helps them stay safe.

The wild boar is the ancestor of pigs that live on farms. Thousands of years ago all piglets had stripes!

ALL ABOUT

Wild Boar Piglets

Time mother pregnant: 110–120 days

Number born at a time: 4–10

First food: Milk

Wild Boars

Wild boars live in forests in Europe and Asia. The adults are plain brown, but the babies have stripes to help them hide under trees and bushes. Baby wild boars follow their mother everywhere she goes. They drink her milk.

Baby wild boars like to stay close to their brothers and sisters.

These piglets are play-fighting. Although they are small, they are noisy and often squeal loudly.

Deer

Baby deer are good at running, but when they sense danger, they usually hide. If they stay quiet and still, a hunting animal might not notice them. There are many different types of deer in the world. Some are much bigger than others.

Baby deer have large ears to help them listen for dangerous animals.

This fawn has brown fur and white spots. Most baby deer are born with spots for camouflage.

This baby deer is being nuzzled by a young male. The only female deer that have antlers are reindeer.

ALL ABOUT

Fawns

Time mother pregnant: 200–300 days

Number born at a time: 1 or 2

First food: Milk

This little guy is hiding in the long grass. He is waiting for his mother. To be safe, he stays still and quiet.

Hiding From Danger

Running away is one way to stay safe from danger. Another way is to hide. Many baby animals have coats that are colored or patterned to blend in with the background. This is called camouflage. Predators (animals who hunt other animals) won't see them if they stay still.

Polar bears' clear fur looks white against snow, helping them blend in.

Can you see these quail chicks? Their speckled feathers look just like the dry grass.

This baby fox's brown coat makes him blend in with the grass, too. It helps him stay safe.

Even baby snakes need to hide from danger. This copperhead's pattern looks like fallen leaves.

Camels

Camels live in some of the world's driest places. As adults, they can go for weeks without water. Baby camels drink their mothers' milk. They have long legs and are able to run with their mothers when they are just a few days old.

A camel's long eyelashes and nostrils, which can close, keep out windblown sand.

This mother and baby are dromedaries. This kind of camel
has only one hump, not two.

This baby Bactrian camel has two humps that store fat. They get smaller when the camel does not eat.

ALL ABOUT

Camel Calves

Time mother pregnant: 360–430 days

Number born at a time: 1 or 2

First food: Milk

Zebras

Zebras are wild horses. They look like horses but have stripes and stiff manes that stick up in the air. Like all horses, zebras are good at running. A zebra foal can run nearly as fast as his mother and stays close to her while she travels with the herd.

Zebras can run within hours of birth. This foal's mom is watching nearby.

In Africa, where zebras live, it is very dry. This mother and foal are drinking at a watering hole.

A mother zebra and her baby like to be together. Baby zebras drink milk until they are 10 months old.

ALL ABOUT

Zebra Foals

Time mother pregnant: 360–390 days

Number born at a time: 1 or 2

First food: Milk

Baby giraffes drink milk until they are a year old. They start eating leaves as well when they are four months old.

ALL ABOUT

Giraffe Calves

Time mother pregnant: 430–460 days

Number born at a time: 1 or 2

First food: Milk

Giraffes

Baby giraffes enter the world with a bump! Their mothers give birth standing up, so they fall about 6 feet (1.8 meters) to the ground. Baby giraffes have such long legs that standing up is not easy. Even so, they walk when they are just hours old.

Baby giraffes are born tall! They are already as tall as a grown man at birth.

This little giraffe can stand up, but her mother and another giraffe are helping keep her steady.

Elephants

At birth, baby elephants weigh more than most full-grown men. But even so, lions and other predators can hurt them. They need to learn to walk quickly so they can stay with the rest of the herd. The adults keep them safe from harm.

This baby elephant is only a few days old, but he is already exploring.

Elephants can use their trunks to suck up water. This mother

is giving her baby a shower!

This little guy is trying to look tough. Elephants spread out their ears to scare other animals.

ALL ABOUT

Elephant Calves

Time mother pregnant: 630–660 days

Number born at a time: 1 or 2

First food: Milk

Cygnets swim behind their mother. Sometimes they ride on her back as she swims. On land, they walk behind her.

Follow Me!

Most baby animals are born knowing they should follow mom. Many need their mothers for food. Baby mammals drink their mothers' milk. Other babies stay with their mothers or fathers for protection. Once they can take care of themselves, they go out alone.

Lambs follow their moms. They call out by bleating if they get left behind.

Even big chicks stay with mom. Soon these Canada goose chicks will start growing adult feathers.

Baby elephants grow up slowly. They drink their mother's milk until they are more than a year old.

This foal is running next to his mom. Staying close makes him feel safer than when he is on his own.

Rhinoceroses

Rhinoceroses live in Africa and Asia. There are five different types—these ones are white rhinos. Baby rhinos are the second biggest land-living babies. Elephants are the biggest. A baby rhino grows fast. It can gain 30 pounds (13 kg) every week.

Baby rhinos only have little horns, but their horns soon grow bigger.

White rhinos first start eating grass when they are about two months old.

Baby rhinos look tough, but they still need mom. If mom sees danger, she will charge at it right away.

ALL ABOUT

Rhino Calves

Time mother pregnant: 450–510 days

Number born at a time: 1 or 2

First food: Milk

Paws & Claws

Most hunting animals are fierce when they need to be, but their young are some of the cutest baby animals of all.

Grizzly Bears

Baby bears are very cute and cuddly looking. Grizzly bears are the real-life versions of toy teddy bears. They are very small when they are born, but they grow fast. Cubs use their sharp teeth to eat meat and fish.

Bear cubs have a great time play-fighting. These two are ready to rumble!

Adult grizzly bears are good at catching fish from rivers and lakes. Cubs like the water, too.

Bear cubs have sharp claws to help them climb trees. If they sense danger, they run up a tree.

ALL ABOUT

Bear Cubs

Time mother pregnant: 180–266 days

Number born at a time: 2 or 3

First food: Milk

Polar bear cubs are born in snow caves in the middle of winter. They do not come out until spring.

ALL ABOUT

Polar Bear Cubs

Time mother pregnant: 190–260 days

Number born at a time: 1–4

First food: Milk

Polar Bears

Polar bears live in the Arctic, where it is often snowy. Their coats look white to help them hide in snow and ice. They have thick fur to keep them warm. When they are young, polar bears drink milk. When they grow up, they eat fish and meat.

Polar bears have black skin underneath their fur. See his nose and lips?

This polar bear cub is following his mother. Maybe he wants to play or get some milk?

Giant Pandas

At birth, panda cubs are smaller than a tube of toothpaste. They are helpless and need their mothers. But they grow fast! Cubs stay with their mothers for 18 months. Pandas come from China and live in bamboo forests. They are very rare.

Mother pandas lick their cubs clean. This baby looks like he likes it!

Panda cubs learn by playing. These cubs live in a reserve in China that protects pandas.

Baby pandas are very good at climbing trees. They use their strong legs and sharp, hooked claws.

ALL ABOUT

Panda Cubs

Time mother pregnant: 95–160 days

Number born at a time: 1 or 2

First food: Milk

Young joeys (baby kangaroos) drink their mother's milk inside the pouch. It's also a safe place to hide.

In the Pouch

Some animal babies are carried around by their mothers in a special pouch. Animals with pouches are called marsupials. Most marsupials come from Australia. Some live in South America and one, the opossum, lives in North America. Kangaroos are marsupials.

This baby kangaroo is peeking out of his mother's pouch.

1 When I was born, I was really tiny. Now I am pretty big. I like to look around.

2 Mom can still carry me around, but it is quite a squeeze. Sometimes I like to climb out.

3 I am too big to fit in the pouch, so I follow mom. There is a new baby in her pouch.

These babies are sticking close to mom. If she spots danger, they will all run and hide in their burrow.

ALL ABOUT

Meerkat Pups

Time mother pregnant: 75–83 days

Number born at a time: 2–5

First food: Milk

Meerkats

Adult meerkats are cute little critters, and their babies are even more charming. Meerkats grow up to be about 1 foot (30 cm) tall. Meerkats are related to mongooses and come from Africa. They live in family groups that are known as clans.

Look out! Meerkats stand on their back legs to see over long grass.

Baby meerkats are curious about everything! Sticking together makes them feel safe.

Raccoons

With their black face masks, raccoons look like cartoon bandits. They eat many kinds of plants and small animals. Often, they wash their food by dunking it in water before eating it. Raccoons live all over North America. Some live in South America, too.

Raccoons are woodland creatures, but many live in towns and cities.

Raccoons love to climb and can scramble up into the branches of trees even when they are small.

This little baby looks ready to play peek-a-boo! His long fur is fine and fluffy. It keeps him warm.

ALL ABOUT

Raccoon Kits

Time mother pregnant: 63–65 days

Number born at a time: 2–6

First food: Milk

Like most cats, cougars are good climbers. Cougar cubs scamper up trees to escape danger.

ALL ABOUT

Cougar Cubs

Time mother pregnant: 82–96 days

Number born at a time: 1–6

First food: Milk

Cougars

Cougars are North America's biggest wildcats. They are also known as pumas or mountain lions. Baby cougars are born blind and helpless. Their eyes open after about 10 days. Soon they want to explore the world with their littermates.

Cougars are born with blue eyes, but their eyes turn brown later in life.

Baby cougars have spotted coats. They learn how to hunt by watching their mother.

73

Cheetahs live in Africa. These cubs have fluffy fur on their backs. This fur falls out as they grow bigger.

Brothers and Sisters

Some animals give birth to single babies, but many, like cheetahs, have litters with several brothers and sisters all being born at the same time. Growing up with brothers and sisters can be fun—there is always someone to play with.

Like kittens, cheetah cubs often rest all snuggled together.

1 At the moment, we are just a few days old. Our eyes have not even opened yet.

2 At a few weeks old, we are up on our feet. We still need our mother's milk though.

3 We love to run and play. Cheetahs are the fastest runners in the world!

Foxes

Foxes are very smart. They can survive in many places, including cities, where they sometimes steal food from garbage cans. Foxes eat many different things including mice, worms, and fallen fruit. They are very good at finding food.

Fox cubs need a lot of sleep, but sometimes a littermate wakes them up!

Fox cubs are curious and like to play. These cubs are coming out of a tree trunk to explore.

Foxes have big ears so that they can listen for danger or for animals that they can eat.

ALL ABOUT

Fox Cubs

Time mother pregnant: 49–53 days

Number born at a time: 1–13

First food: Milk

Leopards

Leopards are big cats, like lions or tigers. They live in Africa and Asia. Leopards are good climbers. Sometimes they pull the animals they have killed for food up into trees. When cubs are small, they drink their mother's milk. Later, they eat meat.

This leopard cub is licking his lips. Maybe he wants a snack of milk or meat.

Leopard moms stay close to their cubs. Like most babies, baby leopards love to play!

When mom is hunting she leaves her babies hidden. This little guy is waiting for her to get back!

ALL ABOUT

Leopard Cubs

Time mother pregnant: 90–112 days

Number born at a time: 1–3

First food: Milk

Lions

Baby lions grow up to be big, fierce animals. Their mothers hide them until they are big enough to join their fathers and the rest of the family. Lions live in groups of about 15 called prides. They live in the long grass of the savannas in Africa.

Even young cubs have sharp teeth for chewing up raw meat.

Playing, running, and climbing with their brothers and sisters help lion cubs grow strong.

In five years, this little lion cub will be a full-grown lion.

ALL ABOUT

Lion Cubs

Time mother pregnant: 95–120 days

Number born at a time: 1 or 2

First food: Milk

Tigers have powerful jaws, but they can be very gentle. This mother is carrying her cub to a new hiding place.

ALL ABOUT

Tiger Cubs

Time mother pregnant: 93–111 days

Number born at a time: 1–7

First food: Milk

Tigers

Just like lions, tigers are big and fierce. Lions live in groups, but tigers live alone most of the time. A mother tiger brings up her cubs by herself. When they are small, she hides them while she goes out to hunt. When they are bigger, she teaches them to hunt.

This baby has not had her eyes open for long. She is very young.

Tiger cubs grow up quickly. This little fellow is only about three months old. He has big paws.

Riding on mom is easier than walking around. Her tummy also makes a great place to sleep!

My Mom Loves Me!

The bond between mothers and their babies is very strong. Animal moms really do care for their young and will put themselves in danger to protect them. Most babies feel safest when they are close to or touching their moms. Baby gorillas are no exception.

Mom takes good care of her baby. She is checking for itchy bugs.

I am a young gorilla baby. I hold on tight to my mother so that she can protect me.

Sometimes I ride on my mom's back. I'm still too young to walk as fast as she can.

My mother picks me up and cradles me in her arms to make me feel safe and secure.

The High Life

Some babies are born high up in trees. Before they can look after themselves, they need to learn to climb or fly.

See the yellow eyes of this chick and her mom? They are peeking out from their nest in the top of an old tree trunk.

ALL ABOUT

Owl Chicks

Number of eggs: 2–18

Time to hatch: 4–5 weeks

First food: Meat

Owls

Some birds, such as owls, eat meat. Owls usually hunt at night. They have big eyes to help them see in the dark. Their hearing is very good. There are many different types of owls. Owls live all over the world.

Adult feathers are starting to poke through this chick's fluffy down.

Flap! Flap! Owl chicks must test their wings before they are able to fly and leave the nest.

89

This little falcon is exercising his wings on a branch near his nest. He will be flying soon!

Into the Air!

When chicks first hatch, some are covered in fluffy down. Others have no feathers at all! They need to grow feathers before they can fly. Learning to fly takes a few weeks, and most baby birds practice in the nest. At first, they are not very good, but soon they can fly as well as mom and dad.

This broad-tailed hummingbird is almost ready to start flying.

1 We are too small to fly out of the nest. Mom feeds us until we can fly on our own.

2 We are so big now, we can hardly fit in the nest. It's time to learn to fly!

3 I flap my wings to practice flying. Soon I will be flying away from home.

Koalas

Like kangaroos, koalas live in Australia and are marsupials—animals with pouches. Once a koala baby has grown too big for the pouch, he climbs out and rides on his mother's back. Later he will learn to climb through the branches alone.

Koala cubs have strong claws on their hands and feet for gripping bark.

This little baby looks cozy riding on his mom's back! Koala fur is thick and very soft.

Baby koalas hold on tightly to their mothers. The eucalyptus trees where they live are very tall.

ALL ABOUT

Koala Cubs

Time mother pregnant: 34–36 days

Number born at a time: 1

First food: Milk

Some caterpillars are brightly colored. The coloring warns birds that the caterpillars taste bad.

Time For a Change!

Butterflies are beautiful insects. They lay eggs. Tiny caterpillars hatch from the eggs. They are very hungry and need to eat a lot of leaves to help them grow. When they are large enough, caterpillars turn into butterflies. The whole process, from egg to butterfly, takes several weeks.

Adult butterflies feed on a sugary liquid called nectar, found in flowers.

1 I attach myself to the underside of a leaf to get ready for a big change!

2 I build this chrysalis around myself. It will protect me while my body changes.

3 Look! I have become an adult butterfly! Soon I will spread my wings and fly away.

Monkeys

Monkeys spend most of their lives in the trees. The babies are even born there. They learn to climb when they are very young. Most monkeys live in South America, Africa, or Asia. Some live with just their families, but most form larger groups known as troops.

Most baby monkeys, like this baby squirrel monkey, have big eyes.

At first, a baby monkey rides on mom. He clings to her fur as she leaps through the treetops.

This little baby monkey is sitting high up in a tree. His mom is looking for food, but she is not far away.

ALL ABOUT

Baby Monkeys

Time mother pregnant: 130–270 days

Number born at a time: 1 or 2

First food: Milk

Baby chimps are talented climbers. Both their hands and feet can grasp branches with a powerful grip.

ALL ABOUT

Baby Chimps

Time mother pregnant: 230–240 days

Number born at a time: 1 or 2

First food: Milk

Chimpanzees

Chimpanzees are our closest living relatives. Apart from their thick hair, they look a lot like us. Baby chimps are smart and playful, just like human babies. Chimps live in Africa. They are found in tropical rain forests, which are very hot.

A baby chimp's skin is light colored. It turns darker over time.

Mother chimps protect their babies and teach them how to find food.

Orangutans

Orangutans live high in the trees of Indonesia and Malaysia, which are in Southeast Asia. They are very good at climbing. Mother orangutans carry their babies everywhere. Normally, they have only one baby at a time.

This baby orangutan looks happy. His short, spiky hair is cute!

Baby orangutans rarely let go of mom. Mother and young stay together for about seven years.

Orangutans have orange fur. The word orangutan is Malay and means "man of the forest."

ALL ABOUT

Orangutan Babies

Time mother pregnant: 227–301 days

Number born at a time: 1 or 2

First food: Milk

Water Babies

Some baby animals are born to swim. They may start life on land, but they are made for the water. Other baby animals are born in the water.

This dolphin calf is swimming alongside her mom. Dolphins are mammals and feed milk to their young.

ALL ABOUT

Dolphin Calves

Time mother pregnant: 340–370 days

Number born at a time: 1 or 2

First food: Milk

Dolphins

Dolphins have large brains and are very intelligent animals. They live in groups called schools or pods and work together to catch fish and other food. Baby dolphins can swim from birth. As they grow, they have little trouble keeping up with mom.

As this baby dolphin and her mother swim, they jump up out of the water.

Dolphins need to breathe air. They do this through a blowhole on the top of their heads.

Orcas

Orcas are large mammals that live in seas all around the world. Like dolphins, they are highly intelligent and hunt together in groups. Orcas use grunts and whistles to tell each other things. They also use sound to help them find food.

For orcas to breathe, they must come up for air every now and then.

This orca calf is just a few days old and swims close to her mother's side.

This young orca and her mom are breaking through some ice to come up for a breath.

ALL ABOUT

Orca Calves

Time mother pregnant: 450–540 days

Number born at a time: 1 or 2

First food: Milk

Humpback Whales

Humpback whales are among the biggest animals on Earth. An adult male humpback may be longer than a bus. Baby humpbacks are large, too, weighing 1 ton (900 kg) at birth—that's as much as a small car!

Humpback whales make sounds underwater that travel a very long way.

This mother and baby are jumping out of the water. This kind of jump is known as breaching.

Baby humpbacks usually stay close to their mother until they are about 18 months old.

ALL ABOUT

Humpback Calves

Time mother pregnant: 330–365 days

Number born at a time: 1 or 2

First food: Milk

My mom brought food back from the sea in her stomach. When I beg, she will cough up a meal!

Dinnertime!

Baby animals need food to grow. Some eat the same food as their parents from birth, but others start with a different diet. All baby mammals begin life feeding on their mom's milk. Some birds eat adult food that their parents bring to them. Others find food for themselves.

Baby ducks and geese leave the nest to feed on grass.

We baby crocodiles need to hunt for food. I hatched with sharp teeth and have no problem catching a meal!

I am a very hungry razorbill chick. We are waterbirds. My parents bring fish back to the nest to feed me.

Seals are mammals. This means my mom produces milk for me to drink. I'll start eating fish later on.

Turtles

Turtles are reptiles that spend most of their lives in water, although they breathe air. They come out to lay their eggs on land. Baby turtles look like tiny adults. It takes them many years to grow to full size. Some turtles live for more than 100 years.

This baby turtle is climbing out of her shell on the beach.

This baby painted turtle rests on her mom's back. They are getting warmed by the sun's rays.

Once baby turtles have hatched, they head for the water. They are clumsy on land but can swim very well.

ALL ABOUT

Baby Turtles

Number of eggs:
1–242

Time to hatch:
160–210 days

First food:
Water plants or meat

Crocodiles have eyes that stick up above the surface while the rest of their body is underwater.

ALL ABOUT

Baby Crocodiles

Number of eggs: 4–97

Time to hatch: 70–105 days

First food: Insects and small fish

Crocodiles

Crocodiles lay eggs with soft, leathery shells. Once they are ready, the babies break out with the help of a special egg tooth on their snouts. The tooth falls off soon afterwards. Baby crocodiles are tiny, but they can grow into giant animals.

Baby crocodiles find food for themselves as soon as they hatch.

Baby crocodiles look cute, but they grow up into big, dangerous animals!

Baby frogs are known as tadpoles. They look more like fish than frogs!

I Grew Legs!

Frogs lay eggs, usually in water. Their babies, called tadpoles, hatch from these eggs. Tadpoles change shape as they grow. This process is called metamorphosis. First they grow their back legs, then they grow their front legs. Finally, their tails start to disappear. Then they are frogs.

This baby tree frog has lost her tail. She looks like a tiny copy of her parents.

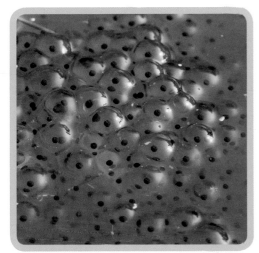

1 Mom laid all these eggs in a pond. Before we hatch, we are called frogspawn.

2 We hatched from our eggs! Now we are tadpoles. See our long tails?

3 I grew up into a little frog. My tail is almost gone and soon I can leave the water.

Baby swans can swim almost from the moment they hatch, but riding on mom's back is less tiring.

ALL ABOUT

Cygnets

Number of eggs: 4–10

Time to hatch: 35–37 days

First food: Water plants and insects

Swans

Swans are large, beautiful waterbirds. Most types are white, like these mute swans, but some are black. Swans eat water plants and have long necks that help them reach down to the bottoms of the lakes and rivers where they live.

This is a baby mute swan. Mute swans come from Europe and Asia.

This little cygnet has no trouble floating. Like his mom, he swims using his webbed feet.

Penguins

Penguins are birds, but, unlike most birds, they cannot fly. Instead, they are good swimmers and spend most of their time looking for food in the ocean. Penguins use their wings as flippers and hunt underwater for fish and other small creatures.

Most penguins have only one chick at a time, but this mother has two.

These are baby fairy penguins. They nest in Australia and are the smallest penguins of all.

Emperor penguins live in the Antarctic. This chick and his mom are with two friends, whose parents are at sea.

ALL ABOUT

Penguin Chicks

Number of eggs: 1–3

Time to hatch: 1–2 months

First food: Fish, krill, and squid

A baby seal's white coat acts as camouflage in snow. As the seal grows, he will change color to look like his mom.

ALL ABOUT

Seal Pups

Time mother pregnant: 335–360 days

Number born at a time: 1 or 2

First food: Milk

Seals

Seals spend most of their time in the water, but they have to come out onto land to have their babies. Seal milk is very rich and nourishing, so seal pups grow up quickly. Some seal pups can swim within a few days of birth.

This baby seal's thick coat helps keep him warm while he waits for his mom.

Mom hunts fish for herself underwater, but comes out to feed milk to her pup.

Otters normally walk on all fours, but they can stand up on their back legs by using their tails for support.

Playtime!

Lots of baby animals play, but otters are more playful than most. By fooling around with their brothers and sisters, they learn skills that will help them survive on their own when they are grown-up. Although baby otters are learning as they play, they also seem to have a lot of fun.

Mom's tummy makes a nice floating raft for this baby sea otter.

1 We were born in a den, but now we are big enough to go explore the world.

2 There is a lot to see out here! I wonder what will happen if we climb on this log?

3 Time for a little play-fighting. We love to run and chase each other around!

Hippos

Hippopotamuses are large animals that spend a lot of time in the water. There are two types of hippo, and both come from Africa. The common hippo is bigger and weighs about as much as a large car. A pygmy hippo is smaller. It's about the size of a pig.

Even as babies, hippos have large mouths. Adult hippos also have long teeth.

These pygmy hippos live in a zoo. In the wild, pygmy hippos live in tropical forests.

Hippos' eyes, ears, and nostrils are on the tops of their heads so they can see, hear, and breathe in the water.

ALL ABOUT

Hippo Calves

Time mother pregnant: 230–240 days

Number born at a time: 1 or 2

First food: Milk

CREDITS

Key t=top; b=bottom; r=right; l=left; m=middle; ALA=Alamy; ARC=www.articphoto.co.uk; COR=Corbis; FL=FLPA; GET=Getty Images; iSP=iStockphoto; NPL=naturepl.com; NV=Natural Visions; PHO=www.photolibrary.com; PHS=Photoshot; SST=Shutterstock.

front cover SST/Eric Isselée; **3** iSP/Eric Gevaert; **4** SST/Karel Brož; **5**(t to b) SST/Shawn Hine, SST/Victor Soares, FL/Malcolm Schuyl, COR/Martin Harvey, iSP/Andrew Coleman; **6** SST/Thorsten Rust; **10t** SST/Simone van den Berg, b SST/cynoclub; **11** iSP/Rafal Zdeb; **12t** SST/Denis Babenko, b SST/pixshots; **13** SST/Caleb Foster; **14t** SST/Mihai Simonia, b SST/constructer; **15** SST/Vladimir Popovic; **16t** iSP/Eva Gargašová, b SST/Kenneth William Caleno; **17** SST/Kenneth William Caleno; **18** SST/Monika23; **19tr** SST/Ekaterina Starshaya, bl SST/Colour, bm SST/Saied Shahin Kiya, br SST/Rudyanot Wijaya; **20** SST/Monika Gniot; **21t** SST/Gelpi; b SST/Lee O'Dell; **22t** SST/Els Jooren, b SST/Yusuf Bin Abdol Hamid; **23** SST/Pakhnyushcha; **24t** SST/Lucian Coman, b SST/Anyka; **25** SST/Olena Zhuchkova; **26t** SST/James R.T.Bossert, b SST/Wendy M.Simmons; **27** SST/Margo Harrison; **28** SST/Daniel Gale; **29t** SST/Vetrova, b SST/Alexia Khruscheva; **30** SST/Marcel Mooij; **31t** SST/mariait, b SST/Melissa Dockstader; **32t** SST/Shawn Hine, b SST/Wendy Kaveney Photography; **33** SST; **34** SST/Joe Gough; **35** SST/Lee Torrens; **36** iSP/Stephen Martin; **37t** SST/Markus Dollinger, b SST/Brenda Carson; **40** SST/Péter Gudella; **41t** SST/Radin Myroslav, b iSP/Dirk Freder; **42t** iSP/Graeme Purdy, b iSP/Derris Lanier; **43** iSP/Lisa DeMore; **44** iSP; **45tr** COR/Daniel J.Cox, bl SST/Jonathan Lenz, bm SST/Bronwyn Photo, br SST/Rusty Dodson; **46t** SST/James Becker, b iSP/Uros Ravbar; **47** ALA/Penny Boyd; **48t** SST/Justin Black, b SST/Elizevh; **49** SST/Victor Soares; **50** SST/Christian Musat; **51t** SST/Atlaspix, b SST/Chris Anderson; **52** SST/Four Oaks; **53** SST/Peter Betts; **54** SST/Kim Doucette; **55tr** SST/George Green, bl SST/aceshot1, bm SST/Kitch Bain, br SST/Justyna Furmanczyk; **56t** SST/Kitch Bain, b SST/Karel Gallas; **57** SST/clearviewstock; **60t** iSP, b COR/Jenny E.Ross; **61** COR/W.Perry Conway; **62** COR/Jenny E.Ross; **63t** SST/bierchen, b SST/Ekaterina Starshaya; **64** FL/Minden Pictures/Katherine Feng; **65** NV/Heather Angel; **66** iSP/Sarah Salmela; **67tr** SST/Kitch Bain, bl iSP/Eric Gevaert, bm SST/Rusty Dodson, br COR/Theo Allofs; **68** iSP; **69t** COR/Paul Souders, b iSP/Amit Erez; **70t** iSP/Robin Arnold, b iSP/Richard & Robin Rodvold; **71** SST/Holger Ehlers; **72** SST/Geoffrey Kuchera; **73t** SST/mlorenz, b iSP/John Pitcher; **74** SST/Gail Johnson; **75tr** SST/Bryan Brazil, bl COR/Yann Arthus-Bertrand, bm SST/javarman, br COR/Winfred Wisniewski; **76t** SST/Vladimir Chernyanskiy, b SST/Carolina K.Smith, M.D.; **77** SST/Karel Brož; **78t** SST/indiagypsy, b COR/Frank Lane Picture Agency/Fritz Polking; **79** COR/Stephen Frink; **80t** FL/Malcolm Schuyl, b FL/Frans Lanting; **81** SST/EcoPrint; **82** SST/Eric Gevaert; **83t** SST/Eric Gevaert, b SST/Helen E.Grose; **84** SST/Jenny Marie Co.; **85tr** SST/Emin Kuliyev, bl SST/Eric Gevaert, bm COR/Randy Wells, br SST/Joca de Jong; **88** SST/Paul S.Wolf; **89t** SST/ethylalkohol, b SST/FloridaStock; **90** FL/Michael Callan; **91tr** NPL/Shattil & Rozinski, bl SST/Cheryl E.Davis, bm SST/Jill Battaglia, br SST/Jeff Krushinski; **92t** iSP/S.Greg Panosian; b SST/John Austin; **93** iSP/Ben McLeish; **94** SST/Darren Baker; **95tr** SST/Marie C.Fields, bl iSP/Brandon Alms, bm iSP/Bonnie Schupp, br iSP/Goran Kapor; **96t** SST/Graham Taylor, b iSP/Michael Davis; **97** iSP/Craig Hale; **98** GET/Anup Shah; **99t** COR/Martin Harvey; b iSP/Gabriela Schaufelberger; **100** iSP/Eric Gevaert; **101** SST/Kitch Bain; **104** SST/openbestdesignstock; **105t** SST/Darryl Vest, b SST/erllre74; **106t** iSP/Eugene Bochkarev, b iSP/Jan Daly; **107** FL/Minden Pictures/Norbert Wu; **108t** NPL/Brandon Cole, b PHS/Oceans-Image; **109** SST/melissaf84; **110** SST/Rich Lindie; **111tr** SST/clearviewstock, bl SST/Vera Volkova, bm NPL/David Tipling, br PHO/White; **112t** COR/David Schafer, b COR/Keren Su; **113** NPL/Doug Perrine; **114** SST/Eduard Kyslynskyy; **115t** SST/Kristian Sekulic, b iSP/Simon Podgorsek; **116** COR/Michael & Patricia Fogden; **117tr** SST/Michael Pettigrew, bl SST/Stefan Fierros, bm SST/Wolfgang Staib, br iSP/Matthew Williams; **118** SST/Karel Gallas; **119t** SST/BPpix, b SST/Svetlana Larina; **120t** iSP, b iSP/Jon Povey; **121** iSP/Keith Szafranski; **122** SST/FloridaStock; **123** SST/Vladimir Melnik; **124** iSP/Boris Katsman; **125tr** iSP/Andrew Coleman, bl iSP/Hanne Melbye-Hansen, bm iSP, br iSP/Rocky Reston; **126t** SST/ylq, b SST/hallam creations; **127** SST/flavijus; **128** SST/Naomi Hasegawa.